Conversations with Bugs

A JOURNAL WITH WORDS AND DRAWINGS

by Gwynn Popovac

POMEGRANATE ARTBOOKS ❖ SAN FRANCISCO

Grateful acknowledgment is made to

John Sanderson, Assistant Professor, Department of Entomology, Cornell University,

and to Alan Kaplan, Naturalist, Tilden Nature Area, Berkeley, California.

Published by Pomegranate Artbooks

Box 6099, Rohnert Park, California 94927

Designed by Gwynn Popovac and Thomas Morley

Printed in Korea

FIRST EDITION

*M*ost conversations with "bugs" begin with "Ouch!" and end with a slap.

Charles Lindbergh might have talked to a fly who shared cockpit space with him during their transatlantic flight, but I suspect that was the scriptwriter's clever way of letting movie viewers hear Charles's thoughts ("You know, ol' chum, the wings *do* appear to be ice-clad.") without having us think he is a crazy man talking to himself.

I sometimes talk to live specimens I have "borrowed" from Nature and carried indoors. "Sit still, eat your flower and we'll be finished by sundown." They of course never make any response that I can detect. This could hardly be called a conversation.

What if we were to go out and sit in the yard or in the field or at creekside with the express purpose of communicating with the insects? Why should they always have to come to us to make themselves known? What about all the insects that mind their own business, and their business isn't us?

When I am able to sit still for a moment in the grass and tune in to the insect sounds (those few my ears are capable of hearing) I feel I'm in a foreign country and don't know the language. Sometimes I get the impulse to try and mimic their chirps and trills and clicks, but this doesn't seem to bring me one note closer to understanding them.

I have a feeling that conversing with insects requires us to use *our* most acute sense, that of sight. Merely focus on a plot of ground, a patch of tree bark or something in bloom, and observe whatever comes into view. One or more insects is bound to make an appearance—it could be fascinating, maybe even dramatic, as well as pleasing to the eye.

Insects do all sorts of crazy things we can't—though we might dream of doing them—such as pupating, and molting, and metamorphosing, and sprouting wings, and mating in midair, or lying dormant for long periods of time, or seeing ultraviolet light, or singing two octaves above high C, and enjoying it.

Insects converse with each other in subtle ways. They can home in on faint scents that originate miles away. They can detect sounds as delicate as dust settling. Some use echolocation, a kind of radar. Some can read disturbances in water waves. Many respond to magnetism. For those who get close to insects, extrasensory communication is an everyday event.

It is appropriate that insects should be the theme of a blank journal. Though volumes upon volumes of intriguing and important information have been written about insects, compared to the astounding number and variety of these creatures, our knowledge of them is a mere speck on a white canvas, a nearly blank journal waiting to be filled.

—Gwynn Popovac

JAPANESE BEETLE—AT REST

While the larva of the Japanese Beetle chews away at the roots of the grass beneath your feet, the adult beetle is eating your roses—the leaves and the flowers. This scarab is common throughout the northeastern United States. It is doing better in its new home than in its native Japan. Name a flower or fruit that appeals to you, and it probably appeals to the Japanese Beetle, too. In large numbers, spreading over a flowering plant, these beetles are a stunning sight, like an evening gown studded with rhinestones.

Japanese Beetle, *Popillia japonica*, Subfamily *Rutelinae* (Shining Leaf Chafers), Family *Scarabaeidae*, Order *Coleoptera*, 1989. Watercolor, black ink and color pencil on paper, 8 x 10 in. From the private collection of John and Jackie LaTorre.

Insects are vital to life on earth. They manufacture most of the topsoil, pollinate most of the flowering plants and shelter the microorganisms that make up the very foundation of our ecosystem.

TO HAVE AND TO HOLD

Damselflies are often seen flying in tandem. After mating, the male clasps the female behind the head. He is "contact guarding" her from the advances of other males, and he won't let go until she has completed her task of depositing the eggs on water plants, which may mean taking a plunge with her.

Circumpolar Bluet, *Enallagma cyanigerum*, Family *Coenagrionidae* (Narrow-winged Damselflies), Order *Odonata*, 1992. Watercolor, ink and pencil on paper, 10 x 14 in.

For fifty million years insects were the sole inhabitants of the air. Then they shared air space with flying reptiles and birds. Insects were airborne a little less than three hundred million years before the invention of the flyswatter.

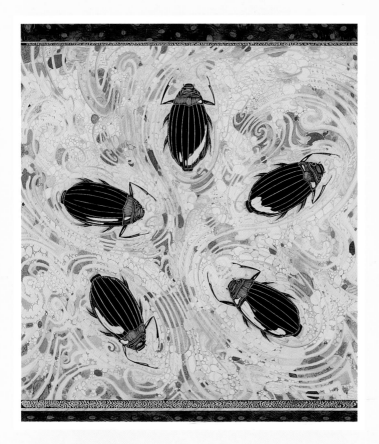

WHIRLIGIG ROUNDELAY

These beetles pass the winter in leaf litter. In summer they can be seen spinning around on the surface of quiet water, like square dancers trying to respond to more than one caller. When they dive they take an air bubble down with them so they can breathe. They prey on insects that fall into the water; they are aided in their pursuit by bifocal vision. Their compound eyes are designed for seeing both through air and underwater.

Whirligig Beetle, *Gyrinus spp.*, Family *Gyrinidae*, Order *Coleoptera*, 1993. Watercolor, color pencil and black ink on paper, 14 x 16 in.

*Of all insects,
only wasps, bees and
ants have stingers.
Of these, only the
females sting.
Stingers are modified
egg-depositors.*

BLISTER BEETLE AND FIREWEED

When pestered, the Blister Beetle has the shocking habit of bleeding from its leg joints. The blood contains cantharidin, a chemical that can ward off birds and ants as well as raise blisters on human skin. Word association prompted me to flank this beetle with spikes of Fireweed. I might have also included a worker bee in the drawing, and shown her taxying a Blister Beetle larva from its birthplace, in the center of a flower, to her own hive, where the larva will flourish on honey and bee eggs.

Blister Beetle, *Lytta nuttalli*, Family *Meloidae*, Order *Coleoptera*, 1992. Watercolor, ink and pencil on paper, 9 x 14 in.

Ants make up most of the biomass on Earth. They outweigh all other animals put together. They monopolize the business of scavenging the corpses of small animals, tidying up the world for the rest of us and making tons of topsoil.

FLIGHT PATH OF A LACEWING

From dusk to dawn, the Lacewing is an aerial acrobat, capable of making vertical takeoffs and executing loop-de-loops, leaving us to wonder whether she's avoiding predators or just having fun. Her eggs, too, appear to defy gravity as they float over the surface of leaves. Actually each egg is supported by a separate filament, perhaps to prevent cannibalism among the hungry hatching larvae. These larvae are affectionately called "aphid lions" because of their appetite for aphids.

Green Lacewing, *Chrysopa spp.*, Family *Chrysopidae*, Order *Neuroptera*, 1992. Black ink, color pencil and watercolor on paper, 11 x 14 in.

A person without a screen door either is homeless or truly loves insects—or both.

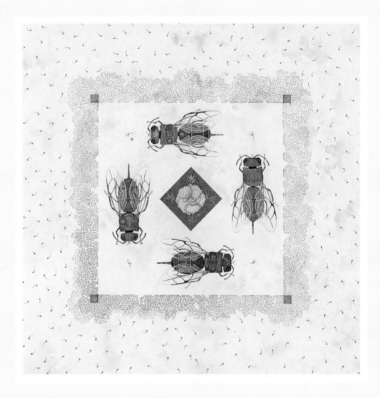

PERFUME MAKERS

The Cuckoo Wasp emits an exquisite fragrance resembling a blend of dianthus, rose and gardenia. To get a good whiff, you must put your nose to within an inch or two of their tiny bodies. Fear not—they won't sting you. They opt for rolling into a ball when bothered, like armadillos.

Cuckoo Wasp, *Chrysis smaragdula*, Family *Chrysididae*, Order *Hymenoptera*, 1991.
Pigment ink, watercolor and interference pigment on paper, 14 x 14 in.

Ninety-nine percent of all species of animals that ever existed have become extinct through the ages. So what's all the fuss about endangered species today? In the latter half of the twentieth century the rate of extinction is ten thousand times higher than normal. Nineteen species of insects are extinguished every hour.

HARLEQUIN BUG BANNER

The Harlequin Bug makes a meal of mustard and related plants: cabbage, broccoli, kale. If disturbed, it produces a powerful odor from glands on its underside. As with the Monarch Butterfly, the South American arrow-poison frog and the Ladybird Beetle, its orange-and-black colors warn potential enemies to stay away and avoid trouble. Harlequin Bug eggs are conspicuous, too: miniature black-and-white striped barrels attached to leaves.

Harlequin Bug, *Murgantia histrionica*, Family *Pentatomidae* (Stink Bugs), Order *Hemiptera* (True Bugs), 1991. Color pencil and pigment ink on paper, 9 x 14½ in.

A good many insects hear with their knees and taste with their feet. If that were the case with humans, we'd all have to wear shorts and be more careful of where we step.

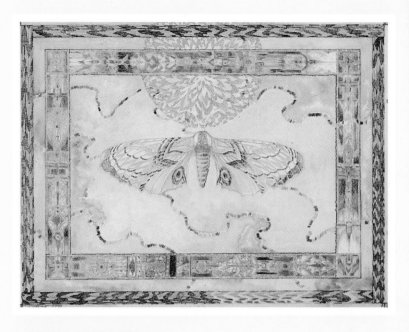

SPHINX MOTH

Motionless, with its wings folded, the Sphinx Moth appears to be a dead leaf or a piece of bark. It will spread its wings and expose the eyespots on its hind wings to startle a molester. Adults of the Sphingidae family beat their wings so rapidly that they are sometimes called "hummingbird moths." But it's the defense posture of the caterpillar that gives the family its name: with its front end reared back and its head tucked in, it resembles the profile of the Egyptian Sphinx.

Cerisy's Sphinx, *Smerinthus cerisyi*, Family *Sphingidae* (Sphinx Moths), Order *Lepidoptera*, 1990. Color pencil and watercolor on paper, 11½ x 15½ in.

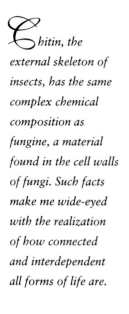

Chitin, the external skeleton of insects, has the same complex chemical composition as fungine, a material found in the cell walls of fungi. Such facts make me wide-eyed with the realization of how connected and interdependent all forms of life are.

VIBRATIONS OF A LONG-LEGGED FLY

Long-legged Flies can be found in wet habitats, running around on the vegetation in search of mates and small insect prey. Their mouths are part spongy bag for securing prey and part chewing, tearing tools. The male performs a slow-motion courtship dance in front of the female. He does not need to offer her a food gift, as many other predatory flies do, because her mouth is too small to be of any danger to him.

Long-legged Fly, *Condylostylus spp.*, Family *Dolichopodidae*, Order *Diptera* (Flies), 1991. Watercolor on paper, 11 x 14 in.

Insects breathe through a maze of microscopic tubes. Air seeps very slowly through these tubes, molecule by molecule. With such a system, an insect with a body much more than three-fourths of an inch in girth would suffocate. Therefore, all those horror films about insects the size of mobile homes are just plain silly.

NET-WINGED BEETLE FLARE

The Net-winged Beetle is named for the fine veining of its forewings. Beetles characteristically have tough forewings, called elytra. They've given up flight power in favor of this armor. The soft elytra of the Net-winged Beetle might well be a midway point in the evolution of flight wings to protective sheaths. I found one of these beetles tucked into the endgrain of an old log, like a bright idea in gray matter. It was only one-fourth-inch long and had a translucent scarlet body, which seemed to glow.

Genus *Lycus spp.*, Family *Lycidae* (Net-winged Beetles), Order *Coleoptera*, 1992. Ink and watercolor on paper, 9½ x 11½ in.

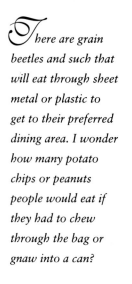

There are grain beetles and such that will eat through sheet metal or plastic to get to their preferred dining area. I wonder how many potato chips or peanuts people would eat if they had to chew through the bag or gnaw into a can?

BLACK PINE SAWYER

Against the bark of a scorched pine, the Black Pine Sawyer is excellently attired for maximum camouflage. This forest dweller lays its eggs in recently dead, cut or burned conifers. The larvae make the sawing sound for which these long-horned beetles are named. Unlike most insects, which have bacteria or protozoa in their guts to aid them in digesting cellulose, the larvae of this beetle family get the job done with the use of enzymes.

Black Pine Sawyer, *Monochamus scutellatus*, Family *Cerambycidae* (Long-horned Beetles), Order *Coleoptera*, 1991. Watercolor and ink on paper, 10 x 14 in.

A solitary wasp will lock its jaws into the stem of a plant and sleep the whole night through like that, with all six legs dangling in the air.

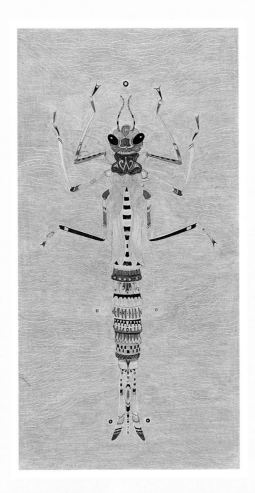

CALOPTERYX

This is the aquatic larva, or naiad, of a Damselfly, as viewed from its backside. Its natural color is a drab olive green—excellent camouflage against the mossy rocks of a streambed. I've taken the liberty of giving the naiad a gaudy costume, keeping true to its real form. From this angle, the Calopteryx reminds me of some zany half-human, half-insect totem pole, of a shaman's rattle for conjuring fish, of a Guatemalan-style Shiva, of a brightly painted metal windup toy from China.

Fanciful Naiad from the Family *Calopterygidae* (Broad-winged Damselflies), Order *Odonata*, 1992. Color pencil and graphite pencil on paper, 7 x 13 in.

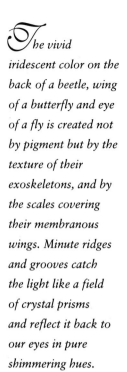

The vivid iridescent color on the back of a beetle, wing of a butterfly and eye of a fly is created not by pigment but by the texture of their exoskeletons, and by the scales covering their membranous wings. Minute ridges and grooves catch the light like a field of crystal prisms and reflect it back to our eyes in pure shimmering hues.

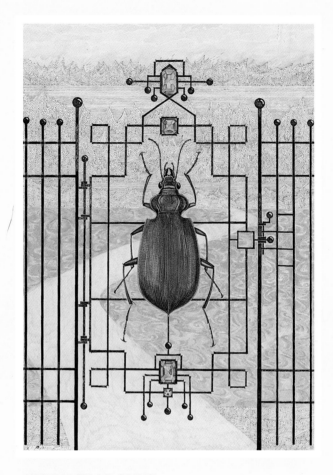

FIERY SEARCHER

This ground beetle is a fast runner, and it seems to be in a great hurry to get somewhere. Sometimes it even climbs trees. The object of the Fiery Searcher's search is the caterpillar, any caterpillar. These beetles lay their eggs one by one on the ground, and when the larvae hatch out they, too, eat caterpillars. When they've eaten enough, they pupate in earthen cells. In wintertime, adults can be found under stones and logs. They live about three years, and in that time they eat about four hundred caterpillars.

Fiery Searcher, *Calosoma scrutator*, Family *Carabidae* (Ground Beetles), Order *Coleoptera*, 1991. Watercolor, color pencil and ink on paper, 11 x 14 in.

With the aid of a strong lens, the wing of a butterfly or moth looks like an impressionist painting—all those scales appearing like dashes and dabs of paint. And like the impressionist painting, the beauty of its color and design can be more fully enjoyed by not viewing it at too close a range.

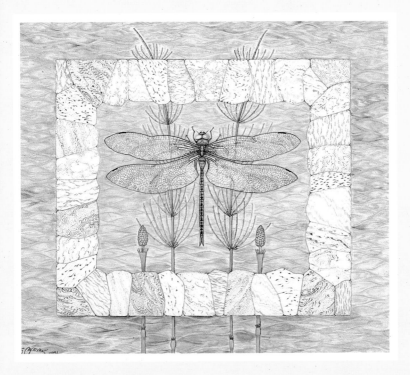

GREEN DARNER

The Green Darner is one of the largest contemporary dragonflies, nearly five inches from wingtip to wingtip. While Damselflies and smaller dragonflies defend limited territories close to the surface of a pond, Green Darners patrol the entire pond from high in the air. They are superb fliers. They snatch flies, mosquitoes and midges out of the air; hold them in their long raspy legs as if in a basket; and chomp on them while continuing to fly around. They even mate while airborne.

Green Darner, *Anax junius*, Family *Aeschnidae* (Darners), Order *Odonata*, 1991.
Watercolor and color pencil on paper, 12 x 14 in.

Sometimes when I sit down on a lush patch of lawn I wonder how many tiny creatures I am smothering or otherwise disturbing. An average cubic inch of soil houses a hundred arthropods. An acre of soil holds a billion.

SCARAB BROOCH

At least one out of every four species of Earth's known animals is a beetle. Over 290,000 beetle species have been named, but the majority remain unstudied, unnamed and even uncounted. Only a small minority of insect species that exist today, and that have existed for eons, will ever be known. In our eagerness to "develop" the wilderness, we are wiping out nearly five hundred insect species every day. I have set the Green June Beetle in a floral brooch, fixed to crushed purple velvet. We put our jewelry away for safekeeping. One day we may wish we hadn't discarded the greater treasure.

Green June Beetle, *Cotinis nitida*, Subfamily *Cetoniinae* (Flower Beetles), Family *Scarabaeidae*, Order *Coleoptera*, 1992. Watercolor and ink on paper, 10 x 14 in.

What builder invented the arch? Those who built the Parthenon or the pyramids? The Roman Colosseum or Gothic cathedrals? No. Eutermes, an African termite, has been building arches and vaulted ceilings for millions of years. Its towering termitaries, scaled to human dimensions, would be as huge as the Matterhorn.

MANTIDS—A MIRROR IMAGE

The Japanese name for the Mantid is *kamakiri*, or "sickle-cutter," an apt name stemming from its swift, scimitar-like forearms. I gave this drawing a Japanese flavor because I pictured two Mantids as Kabuki players holding the I-Might-Strike-at-Any-Moment pose. Mantids are wonderful mimickers of leaves, twigs and flowers. In this drawing, I have done a turnabout and designed bamboolike foliage to mimic the sickle arms of the California Mantid.

California Mantid, *Stagmomantis californica*, Family *Mantidae*, Order *Mantodea*, 1991. Watercolor, color pencil and ink on paper, 14 x 14 in. From the private collection of Robert and Adriana Panovich.

*True Bugs
comprise only a small
portion of the insect
world, one order out
of twenty-six. They
have wings that are
half membranous and
half leathery, and
mouth parts designed
for piercing and
sucking juices from
plants and animals.
If you should say,
"Don't bug me,"
you link your annoyer
to Assassin Bugs,
Ambush Bugs, Stink
Bugs and Toe-Biters.*

A ROTATION OF WASPS

These are solitary Hunting Wasps. The female digs a burrow in sandy soil and drags in a grasshopper she has anesthetized with her sting. After attaching one egg to this food source, she exits the burrow and kicks sand over the opening. The larva feeds, then pupates through the winter, emerging as an adult in summer. Adults drink nectar. I have observed them exchanging positions without contest on umbels of blooming fennel. This constant rotation inspired the drawing, which evolved from pinwheel to doily to mandala.

Steel-blue Cricket Hunter, *Chlorion aerarium*, Family *Sphecidae*, Order *Hymenoptera*, 1991. Watercolor, color pencil and ink on paper, 14 x 14 in.

It is believed that insects evolved from segmented worms: the foremost segments merged into a head, the next three segments arranged themselves into the thorax—specialized for locomotion—and all the other segments became the abdomen. Insect *derives from* cut into. Entomology *is the study of* notched *creatures.*

LONG-HORNED MASKED BEETLE

Could this Long-horned Beetle have evolved a design to humor humans by giving them back an image of their own astonished faces? The pattern is not farfetched; it's typical of the colorful Long-horned Beetles that feed on flowers. The form adheres to the construction of all beetles in this family: exceedingly long, swooping antennae, and a long cylindrical body.

Mascus fanciosa, an invented species, Family *Cerambycidae* (Long-horned Beetles), Order *Coleoptera*, 1993. Color pencil, black ink and graphite pencil on paper, 7¼ x 9¼ in.

Moths are not attracted to porch lights any more than they are attracted to windshields. Long before light bulbs appeared on the planet, moths evolved a means of navigating a straight line by keeping parallel rays of celestial light falling on their eyes at the same angle. Because the rays of local light are radial, the moth is set inescapably into a death spiral.

WOOD-BORING BEETLES

If you pull up a piece of bark from an old fallen tree, quite often you will see a design of some sort etched into the sapwood beneath. Sometimes the design looks like the fossil imprint of some long-legged millipede. Sometimes it looks like a cleverly conceived labyrinth. These engravings are likely to be the artistry of Wood-boring Beetles. Different species create different configurations of channels. Adult beetles bore through the bark, then drill out a chamber and fill it with eggs. When the legless larvae, called grubs, hatch out, they begin gnawing out the many tributary tunnels.

Pine Borer, *Buprestis adjecta*, Subfamily *Buprestinae* (Sculptured Buprestids), Family *Buprestidae* (Metallic Wood-boring Beetles), Order *Coleoptera*, 1992. Watercolor, black ink and graphite pencil on paper, 13 x 13 in.

If it weren't for insects eating other insects, there wouldn't be any room for human beings on this planet, or any other creatures either. Thanks go especially to the wasps, which prey upon almost every other insect in the class Insecta.

A SPECTRUM RED DAYDREAM
WITH GREEN SWALLOWTAIL

This Swallowtail lives throughout the United States, but it's scarce where I live in the Sierra Nevada foothills: in ten summers I've seen only one. I spotted it resting in the shade of a mint bush. When it fluttered off, with its elegant velvet black wings, flashing iridescent green, it looked like a shadow taking flight. Its hind wings are dotted with tiny moons and rimmed with pale crescents. Birds recognize this color pattern and avoid a bitter meal. The pipevine leaves shown in the drawing are food for the Green Swallowtail caterpillar.

Green Swallowtail, *Battus philenor*, Family *Papilionidae*, Order *Lepidoptera*, 1993.
Watercolor, color pencil and pigment ink on paper, 13 x 15 in.

The compound eye of the dragonfly consists of up to 28,000 six-sided facets, each with its own individual lens, giving the dragonfly a mosaiclike total view. This eye design doesn't allow a change of focus, but when put to the test, the dragonfly succeeded in perceiving movement forty yards away. So the next time you see a dragonfly high overhead, you might try waving to it.

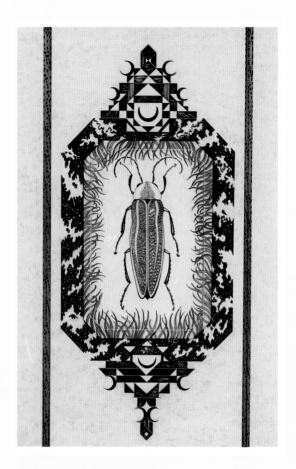

FIREFLY LANTERN

Fireflies are beetles that produce "cold light" via a mystifying chemical reaction in their abdomens. Distinct flashing patterns, combined with distinct flight paths, allow a male and female of a particular species to find one another. In the wetlands of Vermont, where I used to live, there was such a profusion of Fireflies at times that if a person were to step outside into the tall grass on a cloudless, moonless summer night and close his or her eyes and then open them again, he or she might easily lose the demarcation line between the starry firmament and the beetle-lit field, and even have a short-lived sensation of being suspended in outer space.

Firefly, *Photuris pennsylvanica*, Family *Lampyridae*, Order *Coleoptera*, 1989. Watercolor, black ink and color pencil on paper, 14 x 18 in.

Dragonflies possess the ability, unique among insects, to maneuver each wing independently of the other, enabling them to hover and fly in all directions, even backward. And they can fly up to thirty miles per hour without the aid of a tailwind or a thermal updraft.

LADYBIRD BEETLE LABYRINTH

At the end of spring, after gorging on aphids, Convergent Ladybird
Beetles migrate from the lush fields of California's Central Valley to the
Sierra Nevada. They spend the winter together in huge clusters. When
they climb out of their leaf mulch on warm days, it looks, from afar, as
though vermilion paint has been spilled. They return to the lowland
fields in early spring when the aphids are feasting on tender new plants
again. Beetles collected from their winter dormitories and sold for pest
control are not in the mood to eat, and they usually fly away when put
out in the garden. It's as if you or I were yanked out of bed at three
o'clock in the morning and told to eat a seven-course meal.

Convergent Ladybird Beetle, *Hippodamia convergens*, Family *Coccinellidae*, Order
Coleoptera, 1991. Watercolor and ink on paper, 14 x 14 in.

I switched on the bathroom light and there was a cockroach sitting in the sink. He watched me watching him draw his long, elegant antennae through his meticulous little mouth—first one antenna and then the other. And I thought, like the licking cat, the preening bird, and the human with a soapy washcloth, he, too, wishes to be clean.

WIDOW DRAGONFLY—SUMMER NIGHT

With its dark cloak extending over half of its wings, and its yellow striped abdomen, the Widow Dragonfly is easy to identify. It also has the broad wings and stubby body of the so-called "Skimmers." All Skimmers are slow, low-flying insects, dipping often to the surface of still waters to pluck up other small insects. The females drop their eggs into pond water unattended by their mates.

Widow Dragonfly, *Libellula luctuosa*, Family *Libellulidae* (Skimmers), Order *Odonata*, 1991. Color pencil on black paper, 12 x 18 in.

The plumelike antennae of the male mosquito are more than cosmetic. With · them he can detect the humming sound produced by the flight of a female mosquito and direct himself to her. A person in a mischievous mood can create chaos in a swarm of male mosquitoes merely by whistling.

THE BEETLE THEY DIDN'T SEE

Take a pencil, draw some bilaterally symmetrical shape with six legs sticking out of it, and chances are you've drawn some insect that did, does or will exist in nature.

Fanciful insect, Beetlelike, 1991. Color pencil, ink and graphite pencil on paper, 14 x 19 in.

Maybe one day, instead of spraying poisons on insects, people will marinate them—the plentiful ones, that is.

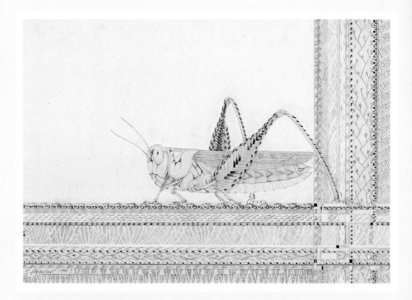

GRASSHOPPER TAPESTRY

This is a species of Grasshopper found throughout North America. They are nonmigrating. I guess they figure, what's the use of migrating if wherever they go they find their own kind there before them? The outer wings of Grasshoppers are narrow and leathery, not designed for flight. The hind wings are membranous, and open and close like a fan. The patterns on their bodies remind me of a finely woven cloth with a grass-and-grain motif.

Differential Grasshopper, *Melanoplus differentialis*, Family *Acrididae* (Short-horned Grasshoppers), Order *Orthoptera*, 1991. Color pencil and graphite on paper

A trip to the nearest flowerbed or patch of grass can be a very inexpensive and exotic vacation. I usually take along a magnifying glass instead of sunglasses.

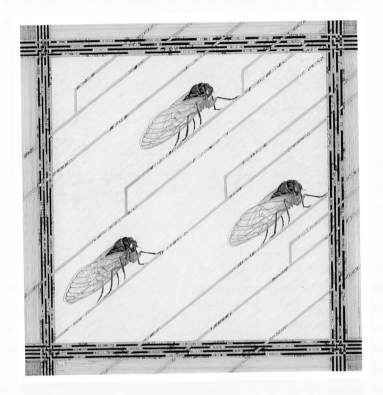

A PULSATION OF CICADAS

The male Cicada has a pair of drumheads on his abdomen, which are vibrated by muscular contractions. Most of his abdomen is a hollow, resonating chamber. The female is silent. Perhaps she is a good listener. In this drawing I tried to make the *audible* visible by transforming the trill of the Cicada into a triad of insects, which, like musical notes, ascend "cords" of sun-hot cadmium yellow. The cords themselves are punctuated with pulses of prismatic color. Sometimes on those seething summer days, the heat itself seems to create the Cicada's song.

Periodical Cicada, *Magicicada sp.*, Family *Cicadidae*, Order *Homoptera*, 1991. Color pencil and pigment ink on paper, 14 x 14 in.